BAT BASICS

How to Understand and Help These Amazing Flying Mammals

Karen Krebbs

Adventure Publications
Cambridge, Minnesota

Cover and book design by Lora Westberg
Edited by Brett Ortler

Cover images: Pallid Bat, front cover by **All Canada Photos/Alamy Stock Photo/Jared Hobbs;**
Basileus/shutterstock.com: stone background
back cover by **kyslynskahal/shutterstock.com**

Photo credits:
All photos copyright of their respective photographers.
David Arbour: 60; **Alex Borisenko:** 32; **Buzz Hoffman:** 44, 46 (main image); **Mark Johnson:** 50 (inset);
Jennifer Krauel: 68; **Karen Krebbs:** 25a, 48, 54, 58, 62 (R inset); 78, 80, 108, 109, 110, 111, 112, 114, 115,
117, 126; **José G. Martínez-Fonseca:** 50 (main image),56, 62 (L inset), 84, 86; **Ken Muir/Kpix Photo:**
62 (main image); **Dr. Brendan P. O'Connor:** 40; **Public Domain/Legionarius:** 64, https://commons.
wikimedia.org/wiki/File:Nycticeius_humeralis_Evening_bat.JPG; **Public Domain/Richard W.M. Jones/**
CC0: 94, https://en.wikipedia.org/wiki/Bat_detector#/media/File:Bat_detector.jpg; **Michael Roedel:** 66;
Karthik Tappa: 72; **Dave Thomas:** 74; **U.S. Fish and Wildlife Service Headquarters:** 25b, 76 (USFWS/
Andrew King), 70 & 82 (USFWS/Ann Froschauer), 116 (USFWS/Marvin Moriarity); **Deb Whitecotton:** 52;
Roger Zachary: 38

Used under license from Shutterstock.com:
Archbob: 13a; **Basileus:** stone background; **Benjamin B:** 12a; **Kushal Bose:** 99; **bt_photo:** 97c; **Dani-**
ta Delmont: 34; **Annie Dove:** 14; **Drifting Light:** 90; **Fredlyfish4:** 97a; **GizmoPhoto:** 23; **Bildagentur**
Zoonar GmbH: 119; **David Havel:** 19b; **IanRedding:** 15b; **IrinaK:** 88; **kezza:** 93; **Ivan Kuzmin:** 9,
18b, 20b, 36, 42; **Marinodenisenko:** 97b; **Roberto Michel:** 19a; **NeagoneFo:** 27; **Carrie Olson:** 13b;
Jay Ondreicka: 46 (inset), 106; **Panaiotidi:** 17; **pemastockpic:** 28-29; **Pranch:** Fun Fact; **Thinnapob**
Proongsak: 10; **Peter Radosa:** 12b; **Jeff Reeves:** 2-3; **salajean:** 16, 21; **Julio Salgado:** 20a; **Salparadis:**
98; **Mary Sisco:** 97d; **StoneMonkeyswk:** 24; **Nathadech Suntarak:** 96; **Sauren T:** 30; **tomertu:** 26;
tuulijumala: world globe; **Jeffrey Paul Wade:** 18a; **Alexander Wong:** 113;
Mr. SUTTIPON YAKHAM: 15a

The range maps are inspired by data from Bat Conservation International, except Rafinesque's Big-
Eared Bat is based on a map from *Bats of the United States*; Michael J. Harvey, J. Scott Altenbach, Troy L.
Best. Arkansas Game & Fish Department.

10 9 8 7 6 5 4 3 2 1

Bat Basics: How to Understand and Help These Amazing Flying Mammals

Published by Adventure Publications
An imprint of AdventureKEEN
330 Garfield Street South
Cambridge, Minnesota 55008
(800) 678-7006
www.adventurepublications.net
Printed in China
ISBN 978-1-59193-843-9 (pbk.); ISBN 978-1-59193-844-6 (ebook)

DEDICATION

This book is dedicated to Kristy K. Mink
who left us too soon but will always live in our hearts.

BAT
BASICS

TABLE OF CONTENTS

INTRODUCTION

Imagine that you can fly. Now, imagine that you are flying at night, through a forest, a desert, an urban area, or above a mountain ridge, and that you're flying without using your eyes! Bats do exactly that! Bats "see" with their ears. They do this by echolocation—a biological system that has a lot in common with the sonar found on submarines. Just as subs send "pings" of sound to detect other vessels, bats emit special clicks from their mouth and use the reflected sound to gain information about their surroundings. This natural sonar enables bats to maneuver, even in total darkness or crowded caves, and it also provides them with vital information about their prey! Better yet, all of this vital information is gained within milliseconds and tells the bat what to do next.

There are 45 species of bats found in the United States. All of them are amazing flying mammals that have special adaptations and abilities that help them survive. They are a crucial part of many different ecosystems, and they provide people with many benefits. For example, they pollinate plants, disperse seeds, and devour millions of insects.

Despite the many ways that bats benefit people, they've been feared and misunderstood for years, and this has led people to persecute bats and even attempt to destroy entire bat populations. Many of the misconceptions that people have about bats are due to superstitions and myths. Bats certainly are nowhere near the threat they're claimed to be.

Join me as we learn what bats are really like. Along the way, you'll experience a bit of what it's like to be a bat. See what bats see (with their ears), taste what they eat, sleep where they roost, fly with ease, and spy on their family life. You'll also learn about the many threats to bats—and how you can help. Bats have an incredible story to tell, and you won't be disappointed in what you learn.

big brown bat

Bat Evolution & Importance

Bats are the world's only flying mammals. In popular culture, bats are often shrouded in mystery, so perhaps it's fitting that their evolutionary lineage is also quite enigmatic. While scientists may not yet know the full story behind their family tree, their importance to the natural environment—and to humans—is undeniable.

Bats serve as pollinators, inspire technological advances, and, perhaps most importantly, play an incredibly important role as insect predators. Along the way, they help out farmers (who might otherwise have to use chemical controls for the bugs) and everyday folks, who can enjoy summer evenings with far fewer mosquitoes.

WHAT ARE BATS?

A fruit bat belonging to Megachiroptera

Bats are mammals, but even though they are often described as "flying mice," they aren't closely related to rodents at all. Instead, they belong to their own order of animals, Chiroptera (pronounced Ki-rop-ter-uh).

There are two main groups of bats, the Megachiroptera (which, roughly translated, means "big bats") and the Microchiroptera (which means "small bats" or "microbats"). As you might expect, bats that belong to Megachiroptera are much larger, and they mainly eat fruit or nectar; they are found in tropical regions of Africa, India, Asia, and Australia. They also don't often echolocate (use sounds to "see"). Instead, they have very large eyes, enabling them to see well.

Bats belonging to Microchiroptera are found in many places, including North America. All bats found in North America belong to Microchiroptera. These "microbats," as they are sometimes called, are what most people think of when they think of bats: small, fast animals that use echolocation to see and to track down prey.

An insectivorous bat belonging to Microchiroptera

With the exception of the polar regions and some isolated islands, bats are found nearly everywhere. Highly adaptable and able to fill ecological niches, today there are more than 1,300 bat species found worldwide, with 45 species normally found in the United States and a few more that show up on occasion or accidentally.

BAT FOSSILS AND BAT EVOLUTION

Bat fossil

Bats are small, fragile creatures, so fossil evidence for bats is rare. Thanks to a few famous finds, however, fossil evidence for bats extends back almost 60 million years. In the 1960s, a small, but complete, bat fossil was found in Wyoming just south of Yellowstone National Park. Many earlier bat fossils were incomplete, but a rare few, like the one found in Wyoming, are well preserved and very similar to modern bats. These complete fossil specimens show bats that look very similar to bats today, with wings that consist of elongated hand and finger bones and ears adapted for echolocation.

In terms of their evolutionary family tree, bats are related to primates, and one popular theory holds that bats' closest relatives are small, arboreal insectivores that could glide, but the idea is not shared by all scientists. However they evolved, it seems bats adapted into their modern form relatively quickly and have changed little since then.

BATS TODAY

Bats play a key role in many ecosystems. Bats provide natural insect control; the majority of bats that live in the U.S. and Canada feed on insects, including many pests. Fewer pests means that farmers often have to apply insecticides less often.

Insectivorous bats hunting for bugs

Fruit- and nectar-eating bats occur in both the western and eastern hemispheres, and they pollinate perennially popular plants such as bananas, mangoes, and agave. Beyond pollination, bats are important dispersers of seeds, enabling forests and other habitats to regrow. Even bat waste (guano) has been used historically, as it's an excellent organic fertilizer that's rich in nitrogen.

BAT BASICS

Anatomy

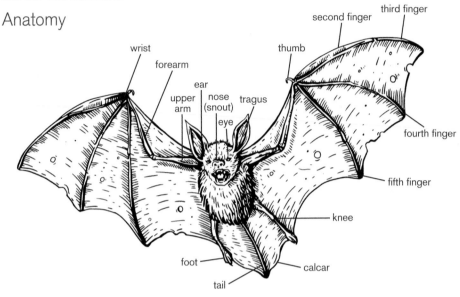

The Hand-Wing: As children, many of us ran around flapping our arms, pretending to fly, but bats can actually do it, thanks to a special adaptation called a hand-wing. In terms of bone structure, a bat's arm and hand are similar to those of other mammals (including humans), but with some important modifications. A bat's upper arm, elbow, lower arm, and wrist lead to highly elongated fingers that make up the wing. The finger bones are long, strong, and supported by struts that take the place of heavier bones, lightening the weight and enabling highly maneuverable flight. The thumb acts like a claw for movement or grasping. The arm and fingers are enclosed in a living membrane that is very strong and damage-resistant and that heals if torn or ripped.

Bats use their wings for more than just flying. Bats' wings help them capture insects, disperse heat to cool down on hot days, and stay warm when it's cold; they even flap them to attract other bats during courtship.

Wing Shape: A bat's wing shape (and flight speed) varies depending on its foraging behavior and intended prey species. Bats that fly long distances for food or when migrating have long, narrow wings that enable them to fly faster and are well-suited to foraging in open areas. Bats that fly in forests or congested habitats have shorter, broader wings, which are more maneuverable in flight, perfect for flying amid foliage, trees, and other obstacles.

A bat wing

Hind Feet: Bats are famous for hanging upside down. They can do this because their feet are rotated 180° in relation to their knees. This means that their knees are pointed backward and the feet face forward, and when they hang upside down the tendons in their toes automatically lock into place, in much the same way that our legs do when we stand. (Birds have the same type of mechanism when they perch upright.) Bats don't get lightheaded or pass out due to another special adaptation: valves and muscles that prevent blood from rushing to their head.

A bat using its claws to hold onto rock

But then there's the question of why bats hang upside down at all. A bat's wings, while strong, can still be delicate, and hanging upside down helps protects the wings. Also, hanging upside down allows a bat to fly off simply by dropping and then spreading its wings.

How Bats Fly

Bats are the only mammals that can truly fly. Flying squirrels, flying lemurs, and gliders don't actually fly; they glide. A bat's wings provide lift and thrust, and flight has helped bats, as a group, expand their territories farther than other mammals.

Bat flight works a little differently than bird flight does. In birds, the flight muscles are attached to a large keel at the center of the chest; however, in bats, the flight muscles are attached to the breast, shoulder, and the back. Without a prominent keel, bats have a much narrower chest, enabling them to squeeze into small areas to hide or roost. A bat's bones are supported by struts, eliminating the need for the heavy, marrow-filled bones found in other mammals. Bats also have very short necks, further reducing weight and maintaining a center of balance toward the core of their body.

To move forward, a bat lifts its wings and moves them backward, down, and then forward, essentially completing a flight cycle. Unlike birds, bats can actually move their wings independently of each other (and even change the shape of their wings as they fly), enabling a bat to have much more control when flying.

A bat happy to show off its long ears

Bat Senses

Hearing and Echolocation: When you see a bat, one of the first things you'll notice is its ears, which are often oversized or unusually shaped. A bat's ears are adapted to make echolocation possible. A bat echolocates by making special high-intensity sounds that are usually beyond the range of human hearing. The echoes of that initial sound are detected by the bat's ears, providing the bat with all the information that it needs to chase an insect or maneuver in flight. When echolocating, bats can detect the shape, size, speed, distance, and even how juicy an insect is. Echolocation may also help bats communicate with each other.

Many bats also possess very good regular hearing. Some species can even detect the sound of an insect's footsteps!

Echolocation for Hunting:
At the start of the echolocation process, the bat is
in what's called the "search
phase," and it produces
around 25 pulses of sound
per second. If the bat locates
an insect, the echolocation
pattern shifts into what's
known as the "approach
stage," and the sounds
speed up to around 50

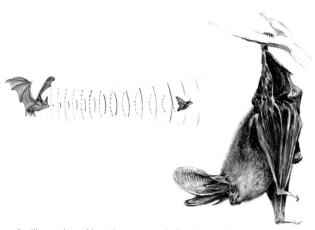

An illustration of how bats use echolocation to find prey

pulses second. Then during the "terminal, or killing, stage," the sounds are produced at 100 pulses per second or greater! This last stage is called the "feeding buzz," in which all of the sounds run together in a continuous buzz. During the entirety of the process, the bat's brain is processing all of the sound information that it receives, much like a computer processes data.

Bats that don't use echolocation, such as nectar and fruit bats, usually don't have specialized ears, though some still can echolocate. These bats primarily orient themselves by vision.

Some bats emit sounds that are within the range of human hearing.

All bats have good vision, but fruit bats have especially large eyes.

Eyesight: Contrary to popular belief, bats can see fairly well. They use their eyes when flying to orient themselves and distinguish between landmarks, including during migration. Bats that echolocate have small eyes, whereas bats that don't echolocate have large, prominent eyes. The flying fox is a famous example; it feeds on nectar and pollen and uses its large, well-developed eyes to find food.

Many bats do not have cones in their eyes—cones make color vision possible—but seeing in color is irrelevant for many insectivorous bats, which are nocturnal. Fruit and nectar bats have excellent color vision, and many are active during the day.

Sense of Smell: If you ever venture into a mine or cave that houses numerous bats, you'll immediately know it, as bat guano (feces and urine) has a very strong smell. Bats have a very high tolerance for such smells and don't seem to mind the strong odors. Bats use their sense of smell to distinguish between prey items, in courtship and reproduction, in interactions between a mother and her young, and in social

Bat noses, such as the one on this Jamaican Fruit-Eating Bat, are often very pronounced.

communication. Some bat species have scent glands in their skin. Glands can be located on shoulders, the face, the muzzle, or in the reproductive organs. These odors help bats recognize their family or signal reproductive readiness. Many of the odors are species-specific.

Diet

Around the world, bats eat a wide variety of foods, from pollen and fruit to insects and invertebrates, with a few species that even eat blood. Generally speaking, however, most bats either eat insects or plant products such as fruit, nectar, flowers, or pollen. Each species often has its own dietary preferences, some of which can be quite specific.

Insects: The majority of bat species, including nearly all found in North America, eat insects or other invertebrates. Insectivorous bats dine on mosquitoes, katydids, cicadas, flies, beetles, grasshoppers, moths, spiders, midges, crickets, flying ants, scorpions, centipedes, and millipedes.

Moths are a common prey item for many insectivorous bats

Some bat species specialize on particular invertebrates, whereas others are opportunists and feed on a variety of insects. Insects are available in large quantities and provide a nutritious diet for bats. Bats can capture insects in one of three ways: during flight, gleaned from foliage, or captured on the ground. Bats may specialize in one or more of these techniques to capture insects.

A nectar-eating bat in South America

Pollen, Nectar, Flowers, and Fruit: Most bats that eat fruit, nectar, or pollen live in tropical habitats, but there are several fruit- and nectar-eating bats in the U.S. These bats occur primarily in the U.S. Southwest, but one species is found in the Florida Keys. They feed on columnar cactus (such as saguaros), agaves, and fruits, but they may feed on insects as well.

Fruit and nectar bats have elongated muzzles and long tongues to access their plant food. Long muzzles fit into the petals of the flower like a lock and key, and the long tongue can reach nectar in the depths of the flower.

A fruit bat covered in pollen

Bats that eat nectar, pollen, or fruit often play important roles as pollinators. Nectar- and pollen-eating bats often end up covered in pollen, and they move pollen from plant to plant. Fruit bats also help disperse seeds, enabling plant growth and promoting reforestation. Nectar- and pollen-eating bats migrate during the winter because their plant food is not available as a year-round food source in temperate climates.

Reproduction

The reproductive system of bats is similar to that of other mammals, with some unique adaptations and differences. Bats usually reproduce only once a year, and breeding often takes place in late summer or autumn. Many males use vocalizations and wing-flapping to attract females. In some bat species, females can store sperm in the uterus or vagina during the winter, and fertilization occurs in the spring. Gestation usually lasts 30 to 40 days. In other species, fertilization occurs during breeding, but fetus development is slowed, and young are born in spring and summer. In such species, gestation lasts eight to nine months. Most bats produce one pup per year, but a few produce twins.

An African bat species flying with a pup

Young bats are called pups, and when they are born they weigh at least 25 percent of the adult mother's weight. Giving birth to a large baby that has wings is not an easy task, and the pup is born rump-first to avoid problems with the wings. Females usually give birth while their head faces upward and the pup drops into the tail membrane. The pup then crawls to a nipple and holds on with its very sharp milk teeth. The thumbs and hind feet of newborn bats are adult size, so they can hang on to their mothers or to a roosting surface.

Newborn pups demand a good deal of food, and this means that the bat mothers have to make many foraging flights. In some fruit and nectar bat species, a pup may hitch a ride with the mother on a flight, but in most insectivorous species, the young are left behind during foraging, as it'd be too difficult to chase insects while carrying a baby.

Pups grow quickly, and they can fly within four weeks. At this time, most young bats have been weaned and will follow their moms to food. Insectivorous pups have to perfect their echolocation skills and put on fat for the winter. This is difficult, and many young do not survive. Nectar-feeding pups follow their mothers to plants and practice foraging at the flowers. At first, they are very clumsy, but they learn quickly.

The young of some bat species can breed in a year, but others take up to three years.

Hibernation

Bats have a number of strategies to survive the changing of the seasons. Some bats remain active and locate food during the winters, while others enter hibernation or migrate.

Bats that hibernate survive thanks to a unique adaptation known as torpor. When a bat enters torpor, it lowers its body temperature to match that of the surrounding

Bats hibernating in a cave

environment, and the bat's breathing rate and heart rate also decrease. All of these changes enable the bat to conserve energy. An extended period of torpor is considered hibernation.

In order to survive for an extended period, bats must gain weight before hibernation, sometimes as much as 40 percent of their normal body weight. This additional fat enables the bat to survive during a long winter, when the average bat can lose one-fourth to one-half of its overall weight.

The location where bats hibernate (called a hibernaculum) is also important, as its microclimate must meet each species' specific needs. Many bats choose a humid location, such as a cave or mine, that also falls within a certain temperature limit. (While bats are often found in caves, they are only found in some caves. Many caves are simply too cold for bats.)

An environment with high humidity enables a bat to conserve water, and a constant temperature range helps prevent bats from freezing. Different species of bats may use a hibernaculum in distinct ways; some bats may hibernate deep within a structure, whereas others may be found closer to the entrance. Some bats also huddle or group together for warmth and to prevent moisture loss. Many bats utilize the same winter hibernaculum year after year.

Migration

Just as hibernating bats require fat reserves to survive a long winter, migrating takes a good deal of energy. Unlike birds, which sometimes migrate tens of thousands of miles, bats are not typically long-distance migrators, but some have been recorded traveling up to 800 miles or more. Shorter-range migration is also common, as many bats will move to more favorable areas if temperature or food sources are a concern; bats often also migrate short distances (25 or 50 miles) between their summer feeding grounds and the location where they hibernate.

In the U.S., some northern species migrate south to Mexico or to southern states where it is warmer during the winter, migrating back north in the summer. Hoary, silver-haired, and Mexican free-tailed bats are among the species that migrate. Migration usually occurs individually, bat by bat, but some species, like the Mexican free-tailed bat, migrate in large colonies of thousands of bats.

Mexican free-tailed bats, a migratory species, leaving a cave

In the American Southwest, California leaf-nosed bats do not hibernate or migrate. These bats stay put during the year, moving to more favorable roosts if temperatures become unbearable where they had been roosting. By opting to travel to warm roosts, this species saves energy. It also opts to forage when winter temperatures are favorable; when it turns colder, the bat sleeps in its warm roost. Roost sites include mines and caves, which provide the optimal conditions for this species to survive during the year.

FREQUENTLY ASKED QUESTIONS

Raccoons are one of the major carriers of rabies.

How Common is Rabies?

Rabies is a deadly virus that affects mammals. It spreads through the saliva of an infected animal, often through a bite. While it can be transmitted by dogs, cats, and even cattle, it's usually carried by wild animals such as skunks and raccoons. It's also sometimes found in bats; only about one percent of all bats have rabies.

The best way to prevent rabies is to never touch or approach an unfamiliar animal, especially wildlife. (You can't get rabies from simply seeing a bat.) While cases of rabies are incredibly rare—there have been only a handful in the past decade—it's important never to take this deadly disease for granted. An effective rabies vaccine exists, but it must be administered before symptoms appear. Once a person displays symptoms of the disease, death is almost certain.

If you never touch a bat, it is very unlikely you'll be affected by rabies. With that said, there are a few circumstances where you may need to test a bat for rabies. If you're sleeping and wake up to find a bat in the same room, assume you were bitten and seek medical help immediately. Similarly, if you find a bat near a child, a pet, an intoxicated person, or anyone else who might not remember being bitten, seek out medical help. When in doubt, seek medical help.

Can I Touch/Pet Bats?

Unless you're qualified or trained to do so, never handle or touch wildlife, including bats. Humans are big, loud, and scary to most wildlife, and bats will bite out of fear or to protect themselves.

Note: *Some of the photos in this book show bats being handled by people, but the people depicted were trained professionals. Do not attempt this yourself.*

A photo taken during the author's bat field work.

What Do I Do If a Bat's in My House/What If I Find a Sick Bat?

If a bat enters your house, it will often land on a wall or a structure inside the house. Put on thick gloves and place a large bowl over the bat, and then slide a magazine across the top of the bowl. You can then transfer the bat outside without touching it.

If you find an injured or ill bat, report it to wildlife officials, but don't handle the bat yourself. (See above for information about rabies.) In most states, bats that arrive at animal shelters, police stations, and the like are destroyed.

What is White-Nose Syndrome?

The most serious threat to bats in the U.S. and Canada is a deadly disease known as white-nose syndrome, which is caused by the fungus Pseudogymnoascus destructans. The disease gets its name from the white fungus that appears on the bat's muzzle and wings. The fungus has killed millions of bats since the disease was discovered in 2007 in New York.

A bat with white nose syndrome

The disease has spread to at least 33 states and seven Canadian provinces. Unfortunately, the contagion has spread rapidly.

The fungus thrives in cold, wet environments and is active during the winter months. When affected by the fungus, hibernating bats awaken in the winter and burn up essential fat and energy. Affected bats often venture outdoors where they die because of the cold temperatures and a lack of food. Health officials and scientists are working furiously to slow the progression of the disease and to come up with a cure. For ways you can help, visit: www.whitenosesyndrome.org

In the U.S., bats are usually associated with Halloween

What are the Cultural Associations with Bats?

For centuries, bats have been surrounded by mystery and mis-information. It's not hard to see why: People tend to fear what they can't see, and bats are active at night. In Western culture, this has led bats to become typecast as evil blood-sucking monsters, but bats aren't viewed as evil or bad every-where. In classical Chinese culture, bats are associated with happiness, joy, and longevity. In other cultures, such as the Maya, bats were important symbols of the underworld. Bats have long played a role in traditional medicine; either bats or their droppings (guano) have been incorporated into a host of treatments. Modern medicine, too, has developed treatments that are based on bats; a compound first found in the saliva of the vampire bat is the inspiration for a new anti-clotting drug that is currently in clinical trials.

How Do I Bat-Proof My House?

When an individual bat is found in a house, it might be because of something as simple as an open window or a door. Unscreened windows and doors allow insects to make their way indoors, too, so screened windows and doors keep insects and bats out.

Colonies of bats often enter houses through smaller openings, such as small cracks or cavities on the outside of a house. These entry points should be filled, but not before bats living in attics or walls are evicted. Eviction should be carried out after the bats leave for the evening foraging. When young are present during the summer months, the eviction should be carried out in the fall, so as to not trap the young or separate them from the mothers. Bird netting can be hung over the cracks or holes

To keep bats from getting into your house, prevention (and closing off access points) is key

during the day, which allows the bats to exit at night. The net is secured at the top and sides, but it is open at the bottom. The bats can leave but cannot return. When in doubt, seek out expert help from qualified and well-informed pest control companies.

BAT MYTHS, DEBUNKED

There are about as many myths about bats as there are bat species.

Bats don't get tangled in human hair. Unlike what you see in the movies, if a bat is flying around your head it is most likely chasing insects, and it knows perfectly well how to avoid you.

Bats are not blind. Bats see as well as we do, although they don't have color vision, which isn't useful after dark. According to recent research, many bats are likely capable of seeing ultraviolet light as well.

Bats are not rodents. They are more closely related to primates than to rats and mice. Bats are also not dirty animals; they have soft, clean fur and spend a lot of time grooming.

Bats aren't especially disease-ridden. The diseases most commonly associated with bats are histoplasmosis and rabies. Histoplasmosis is caused by a fungus and can be found in wet, humid environments like caves and mines. Inhaling the spores of the fungus can infect humans, but wearing a respirator in these affected environments can help one avoid the disease. Bats can also transmit rabies, but if you don't touch, handle, or get bitten by a bat, you will not be affected by rabies (see page 24 for more).

Bats will drink your blood. The vast majority of bats eat insects or fruit. Only three species of bats—the vampire bats—eat blood, but none of these species are found in the United States. And people are not their favorite target—instead, they prefer preying upon cattle and other livestock.

Species Accounts

Worldwide, there are more than 1,300 bat species. They range from the iconic flying foxes, the huge fruit bats from the tropics and subtropics of the Pacific region, to the familiar big brown bats found across much of the U.S.

This section will provide with an in-depth look at 32 bat species in the United States. They include the most common and widespread bats, as well as a few rarer treats with incredible adaptations. You'll also learn about each bat's habitat, diet, and range, as well as fun facts scattered throughout. Enjoy!

GHOST-FACED BAT

Mormoops megalophylla

DESCRIPTION: Medium-size bats with long brown or red fur. Face with leaf-like folds or wrinkles; ears are connected at the forehead creating a pocket below the eyes. Very unique facial structure that gives the bat its common name. Strong and fast fliers.

WEIGHT: 0.5–0.6 ounce (13–19 grams)

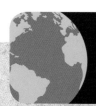

RANGE: New Mexico, Texas, and southern Arizona

HABITAT, ROOSTS, AND MIGRATION: Woodland riparian areas, lowlands, desert scrubland, and river habitats. Roosts in caves, mines, tunnels, and old buildings. Ghost-faced bats are colonial and can gather in large numbers. They don't hibernate or migrate. During the winter ghost-faced bats have sometimes been found in warm roosting sites.

DIET: Large moths and various insects

REPRODUCTION: Breeding is during late winter or early spring. One young is born at the end of May or the beginning of June.

CONSERVATION STATUS: This species appears stable, but more research about its life history and population status is needed to confirm this.

LESSER LONG-NOSED BAT

Leptonycteris yerbabuenae

DESCRIPTION: Medium-size bats with light- to gray-colored fur on top and light brown below. Long nose with a leaf-like flap of skin (a nose leaf), which is typical of many nectar and fruit bats. Long tongue, with hair-like structures on the tip. Large eyes and small, dark ears. No tail. The tail membrane is reduced and looks like an inverted "V." Long, narrow wings provide speed and maneuverability, make long migration possible, and enable the bats to hover at plants or hummingbird feeders.

Even though it sounds gross, these bats ingest urine, which may help in the digestion of pollen protein.

WEIGHT: 0.7–0.8 ounce (21–23 grams)

RANGE: Southern Arizona and southwestern New Mexico

HABITAT, ROOSTS, AND MIGRATION:
Desert scrub habitat and elevated pine-oak forests. They roost in mines and caves. These bats migrate long distances.

DIET: Nectar, pollen, and the fruit of saguaros, organ pipe cacti, agaves, and yuccas

REPRODUCTION: Females give birth to a single pup in summer in large maternity colonies that can number into the thousands. The young can fly within 4 weeks, and they follow their mothers to learn where the best plants are located.

CONSERVATION STATUS: Once listed as federally endangered in the U.S., it was delisted in 2018 and is no longer considered endangered or threatened. Monitoring roosts and foraging habitat remains important.

JAMAICAN FRUIT-EATING BAT

Artibeus jamaicensis

DESCRIPTION: Two faint white stripes stretching from the ears to each side of the leaf-nose. Brown in color, with small ears and large eyes.

WEIGHT: 1.5–1.6 ounces (42–44 grams)

RANGE: The Florida Keys

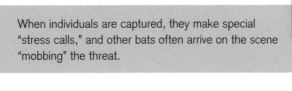

When individuals are captured, they make special "stress calls," and other bats often arrive on the scene "mobbing" the threat.

HABITAT, ROOSTS, AND MIGRATION:

Tropical forests and other areas with fruit. Roosts in caves, buildings, trees, and under leaf fronds.

DIET: Figs are their primary food, but they also consume bananas, mangoes, avocados, nectar, pollen, and insects.

REPRODUCTION: This bat's breeding period coincides with the time of year that fig trees fruit. These bats have a polygynous mating system, in which males fight over and guard numerous females in a harem. After mating occurs in the fall, fetus development is delayed until spring of the next year. This mating system ensures that the young are born when fruit is abundant. One to two young are born in March and April and cared for by the female.

CONSERVATION STATUS: Jamaican fruit-eating bats are rare in the Florida Keys, but they are common in the rest of their range outside the U.S.

MEXICAN LONG-TONGUED BAT

Choeronycteris mexicana

DESCRIPTION: Medium-size bats with a long, slender nose (known as a rostrum). The nose has the characteristic leaf-like flap of skin (leaf-nose) that nectar bats exhibit. The rostrum is longer than that of the lesser long-nosed bat (see page 34). Medium-size ears. Buff brown or gray brown upper fur color with paler fur below. The tiny tail is enclosed by a membrane.

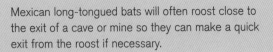

Mexican long-tongued bats will often roost close to the exit of a cave or mine so they can make a quick exit from the roost if necessary.

WEIGHT: 0.4–0.9 ounce (10–25 grams)

RANGE: The southwestern U.S., including Arizona, New Mexico, and southern California

HABITAT, ROOSTS, AND MIGRATION:

Oak-conifer forest, arid thorn scrub, saguaro-paloverde desert scrub, and tropical deciduous forest. Usually roosts alone or in small colonies of a dozen individuals. Mines and caves are the usual roosting areas. This species gathers in small maternity colonies, unlike the Lesser Long-Nosed Bat (page 34), which forms large maternity colonies with thousands of bats.

DIET: Nectar and pollen

REPRODUCTION: One pup is born in June or July; it can fly within three weeks. Once the young can fly, the entire maternity colony becomes transient and the bats move from roost to roost following a nectar trail, a path that follows the flowering and blooming patterns of the plant species these bats use as food.

CONSERVATION STATUS: Considered a sensitive species in most areas, it is important to protect its roosting sites and habitat.

CALIFORNIA LEAF-NOSED BAT

Macrotus californicus

DESCRIPTION: Medium-size bats with large ears and eyes. Brown-gray in color, with a leaf nose. The tail extends beyond the tail membrane. Very agile, with highly maneuverable flight, including the ability to hover.

WEIGHT: 0.4–0.8 ounce (11–23 grams)

RANGE: Southern California and Nevada, southwest Arizona

HABITAT, ROOSTS, AND MIGRATION: Found in Mojave and Sonoran Desert scrub but can occasionally be found in the Great Basin Desert. California leaf-nosed bats don't hibernate or migrate; instead, they depend upon warm roosts, such as mine tunnels or caves in the winter, and must move to another roost if temperatures fall. They also roost in buildings, under bridges, and in other human structures.

DIET: Grasshoppers, beetles, cicadas, sphinx moths, caterpillars, butterflies, and dragonflies

REPRODUCTION: Breeding occurs in late fall or early winter, but the fetus develops slowly until spring. Young are born in the summer after a gestation period of up to nine months.

CONSERVATION STATUS: Rarely studied, California leaf-nosed bats are susceptible to human disturbance. They are a species of concern in many areas.

BIG BROWN BAT

Eptesicus fuscus

DESCRIPTION: Medium- to large-size bats that are light to dark brown in color. The tail is mostly enclosed by the tail membrane. Broad head and nose; the tragus is short, blunt, and slightly curved. The ears, nose, and flight membranes are black.

WEIGHT: 0.5–0.7 ounce (14–21 grams)

FUN FACT

Big brown bats have a heart rate of 900–1,000 beats per minute during flight.

RANGE: Canada and south throughout the U.S. but usually absent in southern Florida and central Texas

HABITAT, ROOSTS, AND MIGRATION:

Found in various habitats, from desert to mountains and everything in between. Closely associated with humans, they are probably the most recognized bat species. They roost in attics, barns, wooden man-made structures, under bridges, and in mines and caves.

DIET: Flying ants, beetles, termites, flies, mosquitoes, and other insects

REPRODUCTION: Breeding usually occurs in the fall, but females store sperm until they ovulate in spring. One pup is born in the summer; the young bats can fly within a month.

CONSERVATION STATUS: Big brown bat populations are stable; they are widely distributed in the U.S.

PALLID BAT

Antrozous pallidus

DESCRIPTION: Large bats with beautiful pale or yellow fur; dark tips above and white below. Large ears, with a long, narrow tragus. The bare muzzle is square-looking with several wart-like glands that secrete a musky, skunk-like odor. The nose is pig-like.

WEIGHT: 0.7–1.2 ounces (20–35 grams); females are larger than males

RANGE: The western U.S. A few colonies live in northern Oklahoma and southern Kansas. They also occur in the southern Okanagan Valley of British Columbia.

HABITAT, ROOSTS, AND MIGRATION:

Arid desert areas, canyons, grasslands, and habitats below 6,000 feet in elevation. Pallid bats are gregarious and roost in small colonies of 20 or more bats. Roosting sites include tree cavities, rock crevices, caves, mines, buildings, bridges, and other man-made structures. Day-time roosting sites differ from night-time roosts.

DIET: Scorpions, beetles, crickets, centipedes, grasshoppers, moths, cicadas, katydids, June bugs, and praying mantises. Pallid bats commonly forage by walking on the ground or flying slowly above it, while listening for low frequency-sounds from insects with their sensitive hearing. It is thought that they can hear the footsteps of scorpions with their keen ears.

REPRODUCTION: Breeding occurs during the winter, and females store sperm until spring. One or two young are born in late spring or early summer. Young can fly at 4–6 weeks and are full-size by 8 weeks.

CONSERVATION STATUS: Populations appear to be stable in the U.S., but this species is rare in British Columbia.

Tri-colored Bat

Canyon Bat

Canyon
Tri-colored

CANYON BAT AND TRI-COLORED BAT

Perimyotis subflavus, Parastrellus hesperus

DESCRIPTION: Two of the smallest bat species in the U.S. The tragus is slightly curved and short. Both species are light-colored, but the tri-colored has dark tri-colored hairs at the base, yellow-brown color in the middle, and dark hairs at the tip. Canyon bats have a dark face and ears, whereas the tri-colored bat's ears are light-colored.

Small canyon bats have been observed entangled in spider webs!

WEIGHT: Canyon bat: 0.1–0.2 ounce (3–6 grams); Tri-colored bat: 0.2–0.3 ounce (6–8 grams)

RANGE: The canyon bat is basically a desert species in the western U.S. and utilizes canyons, rocky areas, cliffs, mines, caves, and buildings. The tri-colored occurs in the central and eastern U.S. and eastern Canada.

HABITAT, ROOSTS, AND MIGRATION:
Caves, mines, rock crevices, and in trees

DIET: Canyon bats feed on swarming insects, such as mosquitoes, flies, ants, wasps, moths, small beetles, leaf hoppers, and others. The tri-colored bat forages on moths, beetles, mosquitoes, ants, true bugs, and others. Both species are usually the first bats seen foraging in the evening.

REPRODUCTION: Both species give birth in June and July, usually to twins. The young can fly in one month and begin venturing out soon after to forage.

CONSERVATION STATUS: The populations of both species appear to be stable.

SILVER-HAIRED BAT

Lasionycteris noctivagans

DESCRIPTION: Medium-size black bats; silver-tipped black fur on the back, giving it a frosted appearance. The fur extends down over the tail membrane. The ears are short, black, and round. Wings are black, and there is fur on the tail membrane.

WEIGHT: 0.3–0.4 ounce (8–11 grams)

Silver-haired bats have been observed roosting in birds nests and woodpecker holes in trees.

RANGE: Silver-haired bats are found from Alaska through Canada and over most of the U.S., with the exception of Florida.

HABITAT, ROOSTS, AND MIGRATION:

Habitat includes woodlands, riparian areas, and ponds. They roost under loose tree bark or in crevices of trees but have also been found in wood piles, garages, sheds, birds' nests, and woodpecker holes. Silver-haired bats are migratory and travel long distances for the winter, and they roost amid stacks of lumber and railroad ties, as well as in trees and buildings.

DIET: Moths, flies, mosquitoes, termites, true bugs, flying ants, midges, and beetles. They fly slowly, and there are usually two foraging periods during the night.

REPRODUCTION: Females have young during June or July. Twins are common, and the young grow quickly. They are weaned at 3 to 4 weeks and can also fly by this time.

CONSERVATION STATUS: Because this species forages and roosts in woodlands, clear-cutting may be detrimental to their survival. But most populations seem stable throughout the U.S.

Eastern Red Bat

Western Red Bat

Eastern
Western

EASTERN RED BAT
AND WESTERN RED BAT

Lasiurus borealis, Lasiurus blossevillii

DESCRIPTION: The eastern red bat is bright rusty red with white-tipped hairs. The wings are black, and the ears are short and round. The western species has orange to yellow-brown fur with white-tipped hairs. Both species have white patches on the shoulders.

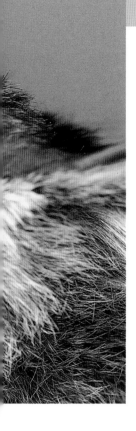

FUN FACT

Red bats utilize winds from storm fronts to reach speeds of 80 mph during migration.

WEIGHT: Eastern red bat: 0.3–0.5 ounce (9–15 grams); Western red bat: 0.2–0.5 ounce (6–15 grams)

RANGE: The eastern red bat occurs from southern Canada and into the eastern U.S. (except the Florida Peninsula). The western red bat ranges from southern Canada through the U.S. west of the Great Plains, and south through Arizona.

HABITAT, ROOSTS, AND MIGRATION: Both species roost in the foliage of trees and large shrubs, usually along streams or rivers, or in fields and urban areas. In the colder regions of their habitat, these bats are migratory.

DIET: Both species are solitary and forage on moths, flies, crickets, mosquitos, beetles, and other insects.

REPRODUCTION: Breeding occurs in late summer or early fall, and the female stores sperm until she ovulates in spring. One to five young are born in the summer. Red bats have more pups than any other bat species.

CONSERVATION STATUS: Both species are common in their areas but are threatened by loss of habitat, such as forests, riparian areas, and woodlands.

HOARY BAT

Lasiurus cinereus

DESCRIPTION: Dark-colored bats with grizzled fur that is frosted with white; the neck has a yellow-tan collar. The wrists and shoulder patches are white. Hoary bats get their name from the hoary appearance of the frosting on their fur. The fur covers all of the tail membrane and part of the wings. The ears are round, short, thick, and black on the edges. The tragus is short and broad.

When hoary bats are found on the ground they can put up quite a fight by jumping or lunging at a threat.

WEIGHT: 0.9–1.1 ounces (25–30 grams)

RANGE: Southern Canada and throughout the U.S. (except the Florida Peninsula and Alaska); populations are also found in Hawaii.

HABITAT, ROOSTS, AND MIGRATION:
They roost in trees and foliage and forage around open areas and water. During the summer months, males and females segregate, and males are usually not found in the eastern U.S. Females fly farther north and east.

DIET: Moths, beetles, grasshoppers, wasps, dragonflies, and other insects. Hoary bats also do not hesitate to prey on smaller bats. The flight is strong, swift, and powerful.

REPRODUCTION: Females give birth to up to four young, but two young are the normal from May through early July. The young can fly in a month.

CONSERVATION STATUS: Hoary bats are common throughout the U.S. and populations are stable. The Hawaiian hoary bat subspecies (*Lasiurus cinereus semotus*) is endangered.

TOWNSEND'S BIG-EARED BAT

Corynorhinus townsendii

DESCRIPTION: Medium-size bats with very long ears (1 inch). The ears curl up when the bats sleep and resemble a ram's horns. Light to dark brown in color, with two large lumps on each side of the nostrils.

WEIGHT: 0.3–0.5 ounce (8–14 grams)

FUN FACT

Townsend's big-eared pups can fly at a month old after birth, and they are weaned by 6 weeks.

RANGE: Much of the western U.S. and western Canada. There are a few small isolated pockets of this species in the eastern U.S.

HABITAT, ROOSTS, AND MIGRATION:

Habitat varies from forests and woodlands to deserts. Townsend's big-eared bats roost or hibernate in caves and mines, with populations ranging from a few individuals to more than 100 bats. They will move around the roost if temperatures change. They migrate but do not usually move long distances.

DIET: Moths appear to be their primary food, and it is thought that there are two foraging periods during the night.

REPRODUCTION: Breeding begins in the fall and continues into the winter. The sperm is stored by the female and fertilization occurs when the bat wakes from hibernation. One pup is born in June. Females gather in maternity colonies of up to several hundred bats. The young can fly at a month old.

CONSERVATION STATUS: Some populations of Townsend's big-eared are declining due to disturbances to roosting and maternity sites.

SPOTTED BAT

Euderma maculatum

DESCRIPTION: Black with three white spots: one on each shoulder and the other on the rump. White underside. The ears are huge, wide, and pink. During rest, the ears curl up.

WEIGHT: 0.6–0.7 ounce (16–20 grams)

Family Vespertilionidae

FUN FACT

The white patterns on the spotted bat's back are very similar to the markings on some moths.

RANGE: South-central British Columbia to the central and western U.S.

HABITAT, ROOSTS, AND MIGRATION:

Spotted bats can be found in rocky, semi-arid habitats and in arid areas ranging from ponderosa pine forests to open desert. It has also been found in riparian areas that are home to cottonwoods, willows, mesquite, and creosote bush. Rock crevices in steep terrain serve as the main roosts; this species usually roosts alone.

DIET: Moths, June bugs, and grasshoppers.
Spotted bats are agile on the ground and can capture ground-dwelling prey, and they also can lift off from the ground for flight. Their echolocation calls are audible to humans but not to moths.

REPRODUCTION: Spotted bats breed in spring, February through April. One pup is born in June or July, and it weighs about 4 grams.

CONSERVATION STATUS: Spotted bats are rare, and their overall population trajectory is uncertain. Additional research on the spotted bat population is needed.

ALLEN'S BIG-EARED BAT

Idionycteris phyllotis

DESCRIPTION: Allen's big-eared bats are medium-size with long tawny, yellow-gray, or dark brown fur. The 1-inch ears have a pair of lappets (flaps) that originate from the base of the ears and project over the nose. The ears can be rolled up in the same manner as Townsend's big-eared bats (page 54). There is a white patch behind each ear. The flight is highly maneuverable, swift, and direct. This species can hover and fly vertically.

WEIGHT: 0.3–0.6 ounce (8–16 grams)

RANGE: Allen's big-eared bats are distributed in the mountains of the Southwest U.S.

HABITAT, ROOSTS, AND MIGRATION:

They are found in pine-oak and coniferous forests, but they can also be found in arid habitats along streams. They roost in caves, mines, and rock shelters. This species is commonly found in areas with cliffs, outcrops, and boulders.

DIET: Moths, beetles, flying ants, and roaches are their primary food.

REPRODUCTION: Males and females segregate during the summer and females gather in maternity colonies. Other bat species can usually be found in the maternity colonies. Maternity colonies have been discovered in rock shelters, mines, and pine snags. One pup is born in June or July.

CONSERVATION STATUS: Populations of these bats appear to be stable in most areas, but it is critical to protect maternity roosts in caves and mines.

RAFINESQUE'S BIG-EARED BAT

Corynorhinus rafinesquii

DESCRIPTION: Rafinesque's big-eared bats have large ears and one fleshy lump on each side of the nose. The brown-gray fur is long and silky with a lighter bicolored area on the belly. This species is very similar to Townsend's big-eared bat. The toe hairs extend beyond the end of the claws.

WEIGHT: 0.3–0.5 ounce (8–14 grams)

Rafinesque's big-eared bats move their large ears like telescopes, waving or moving the ears toward any disturbance or intruder in a roost.

RANGE: The southeastern U.S.

HABITAT, ROOSTS, AND MIGRATION:
Rafinesque's big-eared bats are found in forested areas. Roost sites include hollow trees; underneath tree bark; and in abandoned buildings, barns, cisterns, or culverts. They roost singly or in colonies of up to 100 individuals. They hibernate in caves and mines.

DIET: Moths are their primary food, but they also forage on other small flying insects. Foraging occurs late in the evening; these bats are fast, agile fliers.

REPRODUCTION: Breeding occurs in the fall or winter. The single pup is born in late May and early June in the northern part of its range and mid-May in the south. The young bat can fly at 3 weeks and is full-size by a month old.

CONSERVATION STATUS: Over much of their range, the status of the species is of special concern. Rafinesque's big-eared bats are not common, and they are the least studied of all the bats in the eastern U.S.

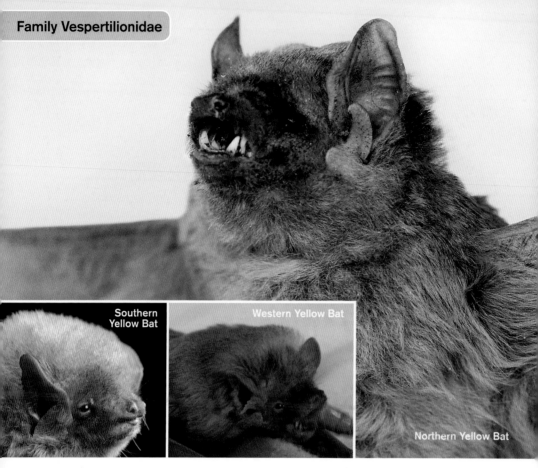

Southern Yellow Bat

Western Yellow Bat

Northern Yellow Bat

NORTHERN YELLOW BAT, SOUTHERN YELLOW BAT, AND WESTERN YELLOW BAT

Northern
Southern
Western

Lasiurus intermedius, Lasiuris ega, Lasiurus xanthinus

DESCRIPTION: These species all have yellow, yellow-brown, or yellow-gray fur. These bats have round or somewhat pointed ears. The southern yellow bat has white on the undersides of its wings. In each species, the fur extends to the upper portion of the tail membrane.

WEIGHT: Northern: 0.5–1.1 ounces (14–31 grams); Southern and Western: 0.4–0.5 ounce (10–15 grams)

RANGE: The northern yellow bat is found along the coastal areas of southeastern U.S. and in eastern Texas. The southern yellow bats occurs only in southern Texas. The western yellow is found in the southwestern U.S.

HABITAT, ROOSTS, AND MIGRATION:

All three of these species are found amid wooded habitats, thick vegetation, and trees. The northern yellow bat is often found near golf courses and airports, and in pastures, grassy areas, and on forest edges. When palm trees are present, many of these bats can be found in palms. In the southeastern U.S., yellow bats use Spanish moss for roosting sites and to bear young.

DIET: Flies, mosquitoes, true bugs, beetles

REPRODUCTION: Yellow bats breed in autumn, store sperm, and give birth from April to July, depending on their location. Two to four pups are born, and they nurse for two months. The newborn weighs 0.1 ounce (3 grams). It's believed that the young bats can breed at one year of age.

CONSERVATION STATUS: The southern yellow bat is rare, but the western and northern yellow bats are fairly common in their ranges.

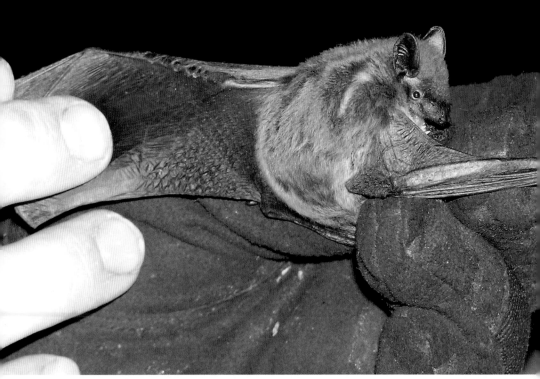

EVENING BAT
Nycticeius humeralis

DESCRIPTION: Reddish to dark brown fur on its back and lighter fur on its underside. The ears are small and dark, and the tail and wing membranes are also darkly colored. The tragus is short and blunt, curving forward; the evening bat is similar in appearance to the big brown bat, only smaller.

WEIGHT: 0.3–0.5 ounce (7–14 grams)

Evening bats have two foraging periods, early in the evening (dinner) and again right before dawn (a snack).

RANGE: Southern Ontario, Canada, and most of the eastern U.S.

HABITAT, ROOSTS, AND MIGRATION:

Evening bats live in tree cavities; behind loose tree bark; and in hollow trees, man-made structures, and buildings. This species does not inhabit caves. Little is known about hibernation or migration for this species. Northern populations may migrate to the southern states for the winter.

DIET: Various small insects

REPRODUCTION: Pups are born in May or June, and twins are common.

Safety Note: This bat was handled by a professional. Never handle a bat yourself.

CONSERVATION STATUS: Evening bats are common along the coast and in the southern part of the country, but they are less common in other parts of their range.

CALIFORNIA MYOTIS

Myotis californicus

DESCRIPTION: Light brown to dark brown with short ears that range in color from light to dark brown. One of the smallest bats in the U.S. Its tail does not extend beyond the tail membrane, its rostrum is short, and its feet are small.

WEIGHT: 0.1–0.2 ounce (3–5 grams)

FUN FACT

California myotis love man-made structures and utilize them more than any other myotis species.

RANGE: Southern Alaska, western Canada, and the western U.S.

HABITAT, ROOSTS, AND MIGRATION: California myotis habitat varies from oak and pine forest to semi-desert scrub; much of its habitat is near water. The California myotis roosts in rock crevices, under loose bark, in hollow trees, and in buildings. This species is also comfortable using man-made structures, but they don't always use the same roosts from day to day. In the summer, the sexes roost separately, but from September to March they hibernate together in mines and caves.

DIET: Small insects, such as moths, beetles, lacewings, mosquitoes, and flies. They fly slowly and close to the surface, often near or over water.

REPRODUCTION: Breeding occurs in autumn, and the sperm is stored until spring. Maternity colonies are small; one pup is born in June or July.

Safety Note: This bat was handled by a professional. Never handle a bat yourself.

CONSERVATION STATUS: The status of this species appears stable. This bat is common in most habitats.

WESTERN LONG-EARED MYOTIS

Myotis evotis

DESCRIPTION: A brown bat with long black ears. The ears are longer (by almost an inch) than in any other myotis in the U.S.

WEIGHT: 0.2–0.3 ounce (5–8 grams)

RANGE: The western U.S. and southwestern Canada.

HABITAT, ROOSTS, AND MIGRATION: This species prefers coniferous forests, but it can also be found in riparian desert habitats and some grasslands. It roosts in small groups (10–30) or singly under rocks; beneath bark; in caves and mines; under bridges; and in crevices, hollow trees, and buildings. Little is known about their migration or hibernation patterns.

DIET: Soft-bodied moths are their preferred food, but they also forage on beetles, flies, true bugs, and lacewings. They capture prey on vegetation as well as on the ground.

REPRODUCTION: Males and females utilize different roosts in the summer; the pregnant females form small maternity colonies. Pups are born in June or July.

Safety Note: *This bat was handled by a professional. Never handle a bat yourself.*

CONSERVATION STATUS: Western long-eared myotis are common, and populations appear stable.

GRAY MYOTIS

Myotis grisescens

DESCRIPTION: Brown to gray on the back and lighter on the underside. This species has fewer hairs on its toes compared to most other myotis.

WEIGHT: 0.3–0.4 ounce (8–11 grams)

RANGE: Arkansas, Missouri, Tennessee, Kentucky, and Alabama

HABITAT, ROOSTS, AND MIGRATION:

Gray myotis utilize caves for the summer and winter, but they don't always use the same caves. Males and non-reproductive females form groups that are separated from pregnant females, which form large maternity colonies in caves in the summer. These colonies can include anywhere from a few hundred bats to thousands of individuals. Maternity colonies are located in warm caves; this warmth enables the young to grow and stay healthy. Unfortunately, there aren't many of these caves available, and it makes this already-endangered bat vulnerable, as the caves can be disturbed and the habitat even destroyed.

DIET: Moths, beetles, flies, mosquitoes, mayflies, and other insects. They usually forage while over rivers or streams.

REPRODUCTION: Breeding occurs in September or October; the females store the sperm until they emerge from hibernation. One pup is born in May or June. The young are able to fly by 3 weeks of age.

CONSERVATION STATUS: Endangered

LITTLE BROWN MYOTIS

Myotis lucifugus

DESCRIPTION: Brown to dark brown with short ears; long hairs on the toes. The fur is long and silky, and it is glossy and paler underneath. Females are slightly larger than males. Also known as the Little Brown Bat.

WEIGHT: 0.3–0.5 ounce (7–14 grams)

Little brown myotis prefer aquatic insects and often forage 6½ to 16½ feet above the ground and up to 3½ feet above the water.

RANGE: Widely distributed from central Alaska throughout Canada and in much of the U.S.

HABITAT, ROOSTS, AND MIGRATION: Highly variable in terms of habitat but often found in temperate forests and woodlands near water. Hibernates in caves and mines and can make lengthy migrations. Gathers in large groups of up to the thousands.

DIET: Many aquatic insects, such as mayflies, midges, caddis flies, and mosquitoes

REPRODUCTION: Breeding occurs in late autumn, and the females store sperm until they emerge from hibernation. In mid-June the female gives birth to one pup, which nurses for about 18 days. Afterward, the young develop permanent teeth and can consume insects. The pups are full size by about one month of age.

CONSERVATION STATUS: *Myotis lucifugus* is widespread and common. A related species, *Myotis lucifugus occultus* (Arizona myotis) is listed as a special concern because of its limited distribution.

NORTHERN LONG-EARED MYOTIS

Myotis septentrionalis

DESCRIPTION: A gray-brown bat with dark wings, a black face, and long, dark ears. It has a sharp-pointed tragus.

WEIGHT: 0.2–0.3 ounce (6–9 grams)

Northern long-eared myotis locate their prey by listening for the wing fluttering of insects.

RANGE: Southern Canada and the eastern and northern U.S., ranging from North Dakota to the East Coast and south to Florida.

HABITAT, ROOSTS, AND MIGRATION:

Found in coniferous forests and various woodlands. Hibernating in caves and mines, this bat can be found singly or in small groups of 100 or fewer. These myotis share their hibernation site with several other species of bats, including little brown bats, big brown bats, and the tri-colored bat. When not hibernating, they roost under the bark of trees, and in buildings, hollow trees, rock crevices, and caves.

DIET: A variety of small insects. They hunt along ridges and hillsides, gleaning insects from the ground, branches, and vegetation.

REPRODUCTION: Breeding occurs in autumn, but the sperm is stored until spring when ovulation and fertilization takes place. One pup (but occasionally twins) is born in June or July.

CONSERVATION STATUS: This species is common over much of its distribution.

INDIANA MYOTIS

Myotis sodalis

DESCRIPTION: A brown bat with short hairs on its small hind feet. A pinkish nose. The calcar, a long spur made of cartilage that is found on the heel of the foot in some bats, is keeled. Also known as the Indiana bat.

WEIGHT: 0.2–0.3 ounce (6–9 grams)

FUN FACT

During hibernation, Indiana myotis bats have a reduced heart rate of just 36–62 beats per minute.

RANGE: The eastern U.S.

HABITAT, ROOSTS, AND MIGRATION:

Found near caves and mines, these bats also roost under loose tree bark. This species hibernates in caves in large clusters of thousands of bats. Hibernation usually takes place from October to April, when temperatures within the cave or mine range from 3 to 6 degrees Celsius (37–42 degrees Fahrenheit) and humidity is 66–90 percent. The bats gain 1–2 grams of a fat reserve before hibernating, as this enables them to survive the long winter.

DIET: Moths, beetles, and other insects

REPRODUCTION: During the beginning of hibernation, sexes segregate during the day, but at night the females join males for mating sessions. Fertilization and development don't occur until spring; pups are born in June.

CONSERVATION STATUS: Indiana myotis bats are endangered species, and they are vulnerable to disturbances while they hibernate. Because there are fewer than 10 known hibernation locations, it is crucial to protect these sites from disturbances.

FRINGED MYOTIS

Myotis thysanodes

DESCRIPTION: A brown bat with long, dark ears and a fringe of hair on the edge of the tail membrane. This is the only myotis that has such a fringe of hair.

WEIGHT: 0.2–0.3 ounce (5–7 grams)

Fringed myotis forage around dense, thorny vegetation and have tougher and stronger wing membranes to protect against tears.

RANGE: The western U.S. and southern British Columbia, Canada

HABITAT, ROOSTS, AND MIGRATION: This species inhabits a range of environments, from desert and grassland to woodlands. Oak and pinyon forests are the most common habitat for this species. This species roosts in caves, mines, and buildings.

DIET: Beetles and moths, as well as other insects. These bats fly slowly, but they are very maneuverable.

REPRODUCTION: Breeding occurs in the fall, but the sperm is stored; ovulation, fertilization, and development don't occur until April or May. A single pup is born in June or July; the young can fly three weeks after birth (sometimes earlier). Females form maternity colonies, but they will move if temperatures shift significantly.

CONSERVATION STATUS: Even though this species is common, maternity colonies are sensitive to disturbances, and efforts should be made to protect these roosts from humans.

CAVE MYOTIS

Myotis velifer

DESCRIPTION: Medium-size bats with dark brown to gray fur, medium-size ears, and large feet. There is a bare patch of skin between the shoulders on its back. It has the long, pointed tragus characteristic of myotis species.

WEIGHT: 0.4–0.5 ounce (12–15 grams)

RANGE: Southern Kansas, western Oklahoma, and the southwestern U.S.

HABITAT, ROOSTS, AND MIGRATION: Cave myotis are very colonial and gather in large colonies of 2,000–5,000 individuals. Habitat varies from desert and canyons to pine-oak areas. Roost sites include caves, mines, bridges, barns, and buildings. Some populations migrate, but others are year-round residents.

DIET: This species emerges before it is entirely dark, foraging on moths, beetles, weevils, antlions, flying ants, and other insects. Diet varies by habitat and season.

REPRODUCTION: Mating occurs in the fall, but fertilization doesn't occur until spring. Females form maternity colonies of up to 15,000 bats. One pup is born in June or July; pups can fly by 6–8 weeks.

CONSERVATION STATUS: Because this species gathers in large numbers, it is especially threatened by human disturbance.

MEXICAN FREE-TAILED BAT

Tadarida brasiliensis

DESCRIPTION: A medium-size bat with brown to dark gray fur, vertical wrinkles on the lips, and broad ears that do not join at the middle of the head. The tail extends beyond the tail membrane, and there are long hairs on the feet. The long, narrow wings enable this bat to fly quickly and for long distances.

WEIGHT: 0.4–0.5 ounce (11–15 grams)

RANGE: The southern U.S., but they appear to be expanding northward into Wyoming and Colorado.

HABITAT, ROOSTS, AND MIGRATION:

Roost sites are selected for their warmth, enabling the young to grow rapidly. Roosting sites include caves, mines, and man-made structures. Mexican free-tailed bats are very gregarious. During autumn and spring, populations in the western U.S. migrate locally and for short distances, but bats from the eastern U.S. make long-distance migrations south into Mexico. During the summer in Texas, millions of Mexican free-tailed bats gather in huge maternity colonies in large caves. Mothers are capable of locating their own young by scent or vocalization among thousands of other pups in the colonies. When the mother rests horizontally on a ledge, the young pup rests on her back.

DIET: Moths and beetles

REPRODUCTION: Mating occurs in February or March; a single pup is born in June or July. Females form large maternity colonies. The young can fly at 38 days and become full-size at 60 days.

CONSERVATION STATUS: Populations appear stable, but because they gather in large groups, this species is vulnerable to human disturbance and pesticides.

BIG FREE-TAILED BAT

Nyctinomops macrotis

DESCRIPTION: A large reddish brown to dark brown bat with huge, broad bonnet-like ears that are joined at their base. The upper lip has deep wrinkles, and the tail extends beyond the tail membrane.

WEIGHT: 0.9–1.1 ounces (25–30 grams)

RANGE: The southwestern U.S.

HABITAT, ROOSTS, AND MIGRATION:

The big free-tailed bat inhabits rugged, rocky canyons where cliffs are available for roosting. This bat also roosts in buildings. It can also be found in Sonoran desert scrub habitats and in evergreen forests at elevations of up to 8,000 feet. It leaves its roost later at night than most species.

DIET: Large moths, crickets, flying ants, grasshoppers, stinkbugs, leafhoppers, and other insects. When foraging, it emits a high, shrill call that is audible to human hearing. The flight is fast and powerful, and the wings are long and pointed.

REPRODUCTION: In the summer, the sexes segregate, and females form maternity colonies. One pup is born in June or July. Very little is known about the specifics of this bat's breeding habits, maternity roosts, the development of the pups, or even the general biology of this species.

CONSERVATION STATUS: More studies are needed to determine the status of the species.

WESTERN MASTIFF BAT

Eumops perotis

DESCRIPTION: The largest bat in the U.S., this bat's tail extends beyond the tail membrane, as in all free-tailed bats. The ears are large, broad, and bonnet-shaped, and they slant forward. The lips are smooth and not wrinkled, and the fur is brown to dark gray. Males are larger than females. The flight is powerful, and the wings are long and narrow. Since this bat is so large, it cannot take off from the ground and requires a vertical drop to fly.

WEIGHT: 2.1–2.5 ounces (60–70 grams)

RANGE: The arid southwest U.S.

HABITAT, ROOSTS, AND MIGRATION:
Rugged, rocky, and canyon-like habitats; roosts in natural crevices and man-made structures.

DIET: Moths, flying ants, grasshoppers, dragonflies, beetles, wasps, true bugs, bees, and other insects. This bat emits a loud, high-pitched piercing call that is audible to humans.

REPRODUCTION: Males have a throat gland that secretes a thick, pungent fluid during the breeding season; it is probably used to attract females. Breeding occurs in spring; one pup is usually born in the summer, but young can also be born as late as September. Maternity colonies are usually small, consisting of fewer than 100 individuals, with bats of both sexes present.

CONSERVATION STATUS: The subspecies of the greater western mastiff bat (*E. p. californicus*) is of special concern, and more information on roosts and foraging areas is needed. *Eumops perotis* populations appear stable.

Bat Projects & Activities

One of the best things about learning about bats is how easy it is to get involved. Whether you're building a bat house or a bat detector, making your yard more welcoming to bats, or visiting a famous bat site to see the bats emerge each night, it's easy to embrace your love of bats!

Build a Bat House

If you want to help out bats, give them a place to live! Purchasing or building a bat house is a great way to support the bats that are already hunting and flying around your neighborhood. Bats eat a lot of insects, including mosquitoes, moths, and garden pests, so you'll get something out of encouraging these insectivores to forage in your backyard. If you're concerned about the possibility of a bat taking up residence in your house, putting up a bat house is a great way to prevent them from moving into your front porch or the eaves of your house. Plus, watching the bats zip in and around your yard is also a lot of fun! If you want a bat house, check out Bat Conservation International (www.batcon.org) for a list of vendors, Bat Conservation and Management (batmanagement.com), Lubee Bat Conservancy (lubee.org), or many bird stores or livestock supply stores. If you are handy with a hammer and nails, you can also think about building your own bat house. Bat Conservation International has produced plans online, which are available on Batcon.org for free. It's important to consult a bat-specific guide like the one listed above (or one similar to it), as it will contain up-to-date research and the features you need to make sure it appeals to bats. Details such as the type of wood, hardware, landing surfaces, paint selection, and location are all important factors for success of the house. You can also make building a bat house a project for your neighborhood, school, or even your city!

Bat House Design Tips

The following tips are inspired by Batcon's bat house recommendations.

Design—The house should be at least 2 feet tall, 14 inches wide or more, and have a 3-6 inch landing area below the entrance. The roosting chambers can vary. Stone and wood structures are good for single-chamber houses. Houses with multiple chambers are adequate for maternity colonies and larger numbers of bats but require more vents. Spaces between the roost partitions should be between 0.75 inch to 1 inch apart. To make it easier for the bats to hang on, the landing and partitions should be roughened horizontally by grooving or gouging them; you can also use plastic screening that is stapled down.

If daily temperatures exceed 85°F in July, the house needs ventilation slots so bats don't overheat. On the front of the house, there should be a vent about 6 inches from the bottom of the house; the front vent should run from side to side and be 0.5 inch wide. If the house has more than one chamber, there should be two (6-inch) side vents; they should be 0.5-inch wide.

Construction—Half-inch plywood is good for the front, back, and roof of the structure. One-inch board lumber is good for the sides. Caulk all seams before painting. All outer surfaces should be painted with one coat of primer and two coats of flat exterior, water-based paint, or stain. Do not use oil-based paints or products. In cool climates (80-85°F or less in July), paint the houses black; in climates with temperatures of 85-95°F in July, paint your house dark brown, gray, or green. If temperatures exceed 100°F or more, paint it white.

Sun Exposure— In areas with average July temperatures of 80°F or less, black houses should receive 10 hours or more of sun daily. In areas with average July temperatures of 100°F or less, the houses should receive at least 6 hours of sun daily. In areas with average July temperatures of 100°F or higher, you should extend the roof of the house to provide extra shade.

Location—Houses located within 0.25 mile of a water source are more successful than those that aren't. Bats also prefer varied habitats, especially those with mixed vegetation or near farms or agricultural areas.

Mounting—Bats prefer houses installed on structures (houses, buildings, etc.) or poles rather than trees. Houses and buildings absorb some of the heat during high temperatures. Mount houses at least 10-12 feet above the ground, and they can even be mounted 12-20 feet aboveground too.

Predator Protection—Install your house on a building or a pole. Bat houses mounted on trees make predation a concern. Bat houses that have openings in the bottom are more difficult for predators to access if they are installed on structures. Predator guards can be purchased from bird stores, if necessary.

For additional details, including diagrams, see www.batcon.org

Landscaping & Gardening for Bats

Bats utilize trees, scrub, rocks, and buildings as roost sites. Tree-roosting bat species like red, silver-haired, or hoary bats, as well as many myotis species, roost in tree vegetation and in hollow trees. Some of the species roost under tree bark. A water source attracts insects and bats. Ponds and swimming pools serve as popular drinking fountains for bats. It also helps if you make your backyard feel more like nature: the more natural plants and vegetation available in your yard, the more likely that you'll attract bats to your home. Don't forget your garden. Night-blooming plants attract insects, and bats will feed on the insects. Finally, steer clear of pesticides/insecticides, which eliminate the main food source for many bats and harm overall biodiversity.

In the Southwest, nectar-feeding bats are attracted to columnar cacti and succulents. Various species of agaves are easy to plant and provide nectar and fruit for nectar bats. Bats are important pollinators for saguaro and organ pipe cactus. In the Southwest, bats can also visit hummingbird feeders at night, so if you put out hummingbird feeders, you might be able to watch hummingbirds during the day and bats at night!

Build a Bat Detector

One of the best ways to teach children about bats is by listening in on bat echolocation. Inexpensive bat detectors are excellent educational tools, and a bat detector, which can detect sounds beyond the range of human hearing, brings the sounds of bat echolocation to life. Teachers and park and zoo employees often use the detectors on nightly excursions for the public, but you can always buy—or build—your own. Bat detectors can be purchased at Bat Conservation International (www.batcon.org) and Bat Conservation and Management (https://batmanagement.com).

Note: They can be expensive. Ready-made kits, which are cheaper, can also be found on Amazon and only require some soldering and a few basic tools. But if you're really into bats, some of the more advanced bat detectors are pretty incredible and can actually identify bats by species.

If you build your own bat detector, you can identify the species yourself by comparing the calls to this chart, which includes some of the more common bats in the U.S.

Species	Lowest Frequency (kilohertz)	Highest Frequency (kilohertz)	Duration (milliseconds)
Pallid Bat	26	49	5
Townsend's Big-eared	21.4	42.5	5
Big Brown Bat	26	33	10
Spotted Bat	8.6	14.5	5
Western Red Bat	38.8	54.6	10.7
Hoary Bats	26	39	15
California Myotis	37	67	6
Long-eared Myotis	54	97	3
Little Brown Myotis	38	78	5
Northern Long-eared	38	110	3
Indiana Myotis	41	75	3
Fringed Myotis	31	49	8
Big Free-tailed Bat	17	30	20
Canyon Bat	53	91	4
Mexican Free-tailed	40	62	15

Note: The frequency ranges above were published in "Recognition of species of insectivorous bats by their echolocation call" in the *Journal of Mammalogy* by M. Brock Fenton and Gary P. Bell. The paper appeared in Volume 62, Issue 2, May 21, 1981.

Turn on the Lights!

You don't need a bat detector to spot bats though. There's a much simpler way to watch bats close to home: Turn on an outdoor light!

Exterior lights will attract insects, and insectivorous bats will often detect them and begin to chow down. The outdoor light source also enables you to get a better look at the bats! It's a simple but effective way to observe the bats in your neighborhood.

If you're feeling really ambitious, consider trying to capture some photographs of your batty visitors. Though be forewarned: Bat photography is notoriously difficult, but that makes it all the more worthwhile!

What Do Bats Eat?

When you see bats flying about, you might wonder what they're eating. Here is a list of just some of the foods that bats eat. Not all bats eat all of these foods, of course, but the combined list is impressive!

Insects—moths, midges, mosquitoes, flies, beetles, termites, spiders, grasshoppers, corn borers, cicadas, caterpillars, dragonflies, butterflies, crickets, katydids, praying mantids, roaches, flying ants, true bugs, gnats, wasps, lacewings, leafhoppers, mayflies, leaf bugs, stilt bugs, stinkbugs

Invertebrates—scorpions and centipedes

Reptiles—lizards

Nectar, Pollen, & Fruit—agave, saguaro, organ pipe cactus, figs, mango, avocados, bananas

Expand Your Knowledge

Getting involved with bats can be as simple as spreading the word about how beneficial bats are to the environment and for healthy ecosystems. But there are many other ways to get involved, and you can help bats out financially too. Some parks have "Adopt-A-Bat" programs where you can financially sponsor specific bats. The following organizations are heavily involved in bat conservation.

Bat Conservation International—www.batcon.org

National Park Service—www.nps.gov

U.S. Fish & Wildlife Service—www.usfws.gov

Bureau of Land Management—www.blm.gov

Texas Parks & Wildlife Department—https://tpwd.texas.gov

Arizona State Parks—www.azstateparks.com

U.S. Forest Department—www.fs.fed.us

The Nature Conservancy—www.nature.org

Sierra Club—www.sierraclub.org

Arizona Game & Fish Department—https://azgfd.com

New Mexico Game & Fish Department—www.wildlife.state.nm.us

The Arizona-Sonora Desert Museum—www.desertmuseum.org

Lubee Bat Conservancy—www.lubee.org

Tucson Audubon Society—www.tucsonaudubon.org/festival

Southwest Wings Festival—www.swwings.org/main-festival

Bat Watch in Austin

Austin, Texas, deserves a special mention. It's home to Bat Conservation International, the nation's premier bat conservation group, as well as two of the best bat-watching locations in the country: the Congress Avenue Bridge and Bracken Cave Preserve.

Various summer events highlight the presence of Mexican free-tailed bats in this area. The Congress Avenue Bridge carries out nightly bat-roost-exit talks by experts and volunteers. Millions of bats roost under the Congress Avenue Bridge each summer. The atmosphere is exciting and festival-like.

The Bracken Cave Preserve conducts special bat flight events in summer. There are Evening Bat Flights, Adult Evening Bat Flights, and Morning Bat Flight Returns. You must be a member of Bat Conservation International to participate in these events at Bracken Cave. Please go to www.batcon.org for additional information.

Other Places to Get Involved

If you're not close to Austin, you're still in luck: many zoos, bird and wildlife festivals, and nonprofits offer bat viewing or educational opportunities about bats.

The National Park Service conducts "Bat Nights" for the public to attend and hosts special activities for children. The Park Service also hires biological technicians for short-term bat work, but these positions are very competitive and usually require a bachelor's degree. Studies focusing on bridge bats are more accessible; they are conducted during the summer and researchers use volunteers to help during the bat fieldwork.

Below are a few ways to get involved.

Arizona

Arizona-Sonora Desert Museum, Tucson, Arizona—Bat Night is held each year on a summer Saturday evening; check the museum's website (www. desertmuseum.org) for details.

Southwest Wings Festival, Sierra Vista, Arizona—During July and August, Southwest Wings hosts a four-day bird and wildlife festival. At the festival, there is a field trip to a Nature Conservancy Preserve to observe nectar bats at hummingbird feeders, and there are bat talks that are open to the public.

Southeast Arizona Birding Festival, Tucson, Arizona—The Tucson Audubon Society conducts a five-day birding and wildlife festival in August. It includes a trip to a local bridge to observe Mexican Free-tailed bats exiting the bridge, as well as public bat talks.

Kartchner Caverns State Park, Benson, Arizona—This park is home to the largest maternity colony of Cave Myotis bats. Visitors can tour the cave, but only when the bats aren't present (October to March).

Arizona Game & Fish Department, Phoenix, Arizona—The Arizona Game & Fish Department conducts "Bat Netting Workshops" for the public once a month during May, July, and August of each year.

New Mexico

Carlsbad Caverns State Park, Carlsbad, New Mexico— "Bat Flight Programs" are held from late May to October. The public can observe the bats exiting the cave with interpretation from a park ranger.

Florida

Lubee Bat Conservancy, Gainesville, Florida—Lubee conducts tours and educational outreach for bats. There are more than 200 bats at this conservancy. They also celebrate "Bat Appreciation Day."

FIND THE BATS NEAR YOU

GHOST-FACED BAT
Mormoops megalophylla

see page 32

LESSER LONG-NOSED BAT
Leptonycteris yerbabuenae

see page 34

JAMAICAN FRUIT-EATING BAT
Artibeus jamaicensis

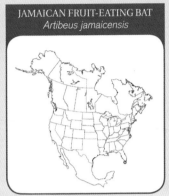

see page 36

MEXICAN LONG-TONGUED BAT
Choeronycteris mexicana

see page 38

CALIFORNIA LEAF-NOSED BAT
Macrotus californicus

see page 40

BIG BROWN BAT
Eptesicus fuscus

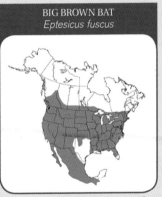

see page 42

PALLID BAT
Antrozous pallidus

see page 44

TRI-COLORED BAT
Perimyotis subflavus

see page 46

CANYON BAT
Parastrellus hesperus

see page 46

This book contains 32 of the most common bat species in North America.
To find the bat species near you, just consult these maps!

SILVER-HAIRED BAT
Lasionycteris noctivagans

see page 48

EASTERN RED BAT
Lasiurus borealis

see page 50

WESTERN RED BAT
Lasiurus blossevillii

see page 50

HOARY BAT
Lasiurus cinereus

see page 52

TOWNSEND'S BIG-EARED BAT
Corynorhinus townsendii

see page 54

SPOTTED BAT
Euderma maculatum

see page 56

ALLEN'S BIG-EARED BAT
Idionycteris phyllotis

see page 58

RAFINESQUE'S BIG-EARED BAT
Corynorhinus rafinesquii

see page 60

SOUTHERN YELLOW BAT
Lasiuris ega

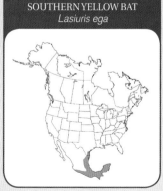

see page 62

FIND THE BATS NEAR YOU (CONTINUED)

NORTHERN YELLOW BAT
Lasiurus intermedius

see page 62

WESTERN YELLOW BAT
Lasiurus xanthinus

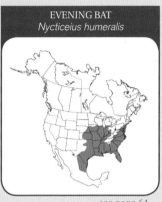

see page 62

EVENING BAT
Nycticeius humeralis

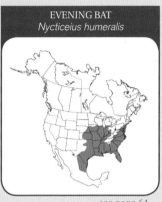

see page 64

CALIFORNIA MYOTIS
Myotis californicus

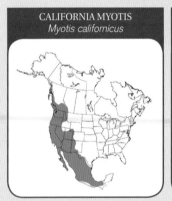

see page 66

WESTERN LONG-EARED MYOTIS
Myotis evotis

see page 68

GRAY MYOTIS
Myotis grisescens

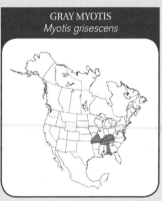

see page 70

LITTLE BROWN MYOTIS
Myotis lucifugus

see page 72

NORTHERN LONG-EARED MYOTIS
Myotis septentrionalis

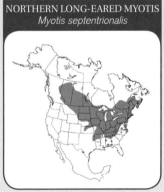

see page 74

INDIANA MYOTIS
Myotis sodalis

see page 76

FRINGED MYOTIS
Myotis thysanodes

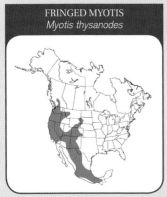

see page 78

CAVE MYOTIS
Myotis velifer

see page 80

MEXICAN FREE-TAILED BAT
Tadarida brasiliensis

see page 82

BIG FREE-TAILED BAT
Nyctinomops macrotis

see page 84

WESTERN MASTIFF BAT
Eumops perotis

see page 86

Ask a Bat
Researcher

Karen Krebbs has been studying bats for decades. One of her studies has been running for an incredible 20 years in a row. To give readers an idea of what it's like to be a bat researcher, how to become one, and the daily life of field work, editor Brett Ortler briefly interviewed Karen to give readers a look at what life is like as a bat researcher.

ASK A BAT RESEARCHER

The author in the field

1. Tell Us About Yourself. Give Us a Brief Bio. I grew up having animals around all the time. I actually wanted to be a veterinarian when I grew up, but I changed my mind when I saw how animals react to vets. Unfortunately, animals have a fear of vets, so I decided to be a biologist. I attended the University of Arizona and received a degree in Wildlife and Fisheries Science. After graduating from college, I spent more than 10 years as a bird and mammal keeper in the Mammalogy and Ornithology Department at the Arizona-Sonora Desert Museum in Tucson. I later transferred into the research department at the Desert Museum and spent 15 years studying birds and mammals of the Sonoran Desert. I worked at the Desert Museum for more than 26 years, and I now work as a private contract biologist. The majority of my research is working with The National Park Service while studying bats. I enjoy hiking, camping, photography, birding, and taking natural history trips.

2. Why Are Bats Important to You? Bats are so unique: they are mammals and they fly! They utilize acoustics, vision, olfaction (smell), touch, and many other cues for foraging, social interactions, reproduction, hibernation, and migration. Their echolocation is amazing and far exceeds technology that we have today. Their diet is diverse and includes insects, plants, fruit, fish, frogs, scorpions, and, in some species, blood! Their reproductive systems allow bats to breed and give birth when conditions are ideal for survival. They are the second-most abundant mammal species in the world. Bats continue to amaze me each day and I am constantly learning new things. I strive to educate others on the importance of having bats in our world. The world would be in a bad place without the many benefits that bats provide.

3. How Did You Become a Bat Researcher? While I was attending college, I fell in love with bats. Field trips were common during the mammalogy class and I began to hang around "bat people." Several of the professors and staff at the college were studying bats. I volunteered my time to help these scientists and my desire to study bats increased. I was amazed at every aspect of bats and wanted to study them. Soon, I was hooked! I have been studying bats for more than 35 years.

4. If Someone Wanted to Study Bats, What Should They Study, and How Can They Get Involved? A good background in biology and science is a good start for studying bats. Early on, children can join a 4-H Club. When I attended college, the University of Arizona was one of the forerunners in wildlife studies in the United States. Their wildlife department was outstanding and

A bat being examined at a study

I took advantage of the unique knowledge that existed. Wildlife and biology degrees are excellent, and you should research colleges and the bat programs that are available. You should also volunteer with wildlife professors and graduate students who are studying bats and make yourself available on research trips. Most zoological institutions have intern and volunteer positions that will give you valuable experience and working knowledge. The more experience you can gain, the better.

5. What Other Kind of Work Have You Done? While attending college, I worked at a veterinarian clinic, at a kennel, on a dairy farm, and on a horse farm. I gained valuable experience working with a variety of animals. While working at the Desert Museum, I worked as an animal keeper, supervisor, curator, researcher, and educator. As a researcher, I have carried out bat research in Arizona and throughout Mexico. I also have led and co-led natural history trips to Mexico, Baja, Costa Rica, Africa, Ecuador, and the Galapagos. As an educator, I conduct talks and workshops on birds and mammals. I also lead bat and bird tours.

6. As a Bat Researcher, Aren't You Worried About Rabies? If you try to touch or handle a wild animal, it will most likely bite you. Even though some mammals contract rabies, only a very few do. Only around one percent of bats have rabies, and if you don't touch a wild animal you'll almost certainly never contract rabies. Like other people who work with wild animals, bat biologists must receive a series of rabies shots, which provide extra protection from a rabies. Bat biologists also take common-sense precautions when working with bats. We wear gloves and follow a protocol, so I don't worry about contracting rabies. With that said, please do not ever touch wildlife. Instead, contact wildlife authorities if you find abandoned or injured wildlife, including bats.

Bat researchers take precautions

7. When You're Doing Bat Research, Do You Get Bitten? When I carry out my bat research I always wear leather gloves; when I train researchers they also wear gloves to handle bats. Bats will bite, but it is not because they are vicious or aggressive. Instead, they are just scared. Humans are big and scary; you might bite, too, if some huge monster grabbed you. Even when wearing gloves, you can still feel a bite from some of the larger bats, but the gloves prevent any injury from the bites.

8. What's Your Favorite Kind of Bat, and Why? I have handled many bats over the past 35 years and each species is special. I love the large bats, such as the mastiff (page 86), big free-tailed (page 84), lesser long-nosed (page 34), or Mexican long-tongued bats (page 38) because they are gentle and rarely bite. Then there are the small bats such as the canyon (page 46), California myotis (page 66), or western small-footed bats that also rarely bite because their mouths are so small. Even the feisty bat species, such as the big brown (page 42), the hoary (page 52), the silver-haired (page 48), or the pallid bat (page 44) have a spirit that is admirable. Hoary bats are huge and make a clicking noise and jerk and thrash around when captured.

Sometimes you encounter bats you don't expect. I was in Sonora, Mexico, carrying out bat fieldwork at a mine when we captured a small reddish-colored bat. It is always exciting to work in Mexico because there are so many different species, and this was a species—Davy's naked-backed bat—that hadn't been spotted during the research project before. The beautiful bat had silky red fur on the head and underparts and a totally naked back! What a treat! Such bats are usually found elsewhere in Mexico and further south to Central Brazil.

Sometimes the bats seemingly want to study us! When I carried out research on nectar bats in southern Arizona, it was not uncommon to have lesser long-nosed bats approach me as I was walking back to camp. I would stop walking and the bat would hover in front of my face and circle me, as if it was curious and checking me out. Then the bat would fly away. Pretty cool! During one winter, we captured male Townsend's big-eared and Allen's lappet-browed bats at the same time and in the same portion of the net. We made sure we released them together after gathering data, because it seemed they were friends and flying around together.

9. How Do You Go About Researching Bats? What is the Fieldwork Like? What Equipment Do You Use? Describe Your Average Field-work Weekend.

Bat biologists utilize several methods to study bats in the wild. I like to set up nets over streams or sources of water to capture bats. Bats use water sources to drink, capture insects, and as flyways. The nets are stretched

Relaxing at camp

between two poles on opposite sides of the water source. The bats become entangled in the net as they fly along the water source. Once we remove the bats from the net, we record data such as species, sex, weight, reproductive status, and the bat's general health conditions. During my research on lesser long-nosed bats, I utilized night-vision goggles to spy on the behavior of nectar bats. The night-vision goggles are heavy and the researcher usually sits in a lawn chair or chaise lounge so their neck is supported. Many researchers utilize special machines to record bat calls and echolocation. The equipment is expensive and sophisticated, but these bat detectors can be set out in the wilderness for hours at a time to record bats. The data is then downloaded on a computer and analyzed. Researchers also utilize video cameras to count bats as they exit a roost. Many exit counts are carried out in this manner.

As a bat biologist, I spend a lot of time in the field. My field day consists of cleaning equipment (scale, rulers, portable table, holding bags, nets), checking all gear, gathering needed supplies (bags, data sheets, species ID guides, antiseptic wipes, camera, bat detector), and getting nets, poles, rope, and pole stakes. It may take hours to drive to the study site, so you leave in early afternoon for the trip. Two to three nets are set up over water before dark and kept open for 2-6 hours, depending on bat activity. During this time, I also train and monitor trainees during the bat capture. At the end of the evening, nets are taken down, gear gathered, and we hike to vehicles. I love field work!

The lovely Desert Southwest

10. Do You Have Any Funny Bat Stories? Or Strange Stories From When You Were Out In the Field? I was working with a University of Arizona bat biologist in the White Mountains of Arizona. We were working with Forest Service employees. At night we netted bats and during the day the Forest Service employees and the University of Arizona biologist monitored rodent traps. They were gathering data on rodent species in the mountains. One morning as I was sitting in camp, reading, the Forest Service employees and biologist marched into the forest to check rodent traps. I happened to look up to see a gray fox following them. The researchers walked in a single-line, one after the other, and the fox brought up the rear! The fox acted as if it was perfectly normal to join the group. I asked them later if they ever realized the fox was there and they replied, "What fox?"

Another time I was working in the Huachuca Mountains monitoring agaves at night for nectar bat activity. Luke Air Force Base had hired me to determine if the military's jets were bothering the endangered bats as they fed at agaves. I was sitting in a lawn chair at the foot of a large hill with a lot of trees. I heard something big running down the hill through the trees. I figured whatever it was would see me, but as it approached closer I stood up to make my presence obvious. A very large white-tailed deer buck was racing toward me! I lifted my arms and shouted, and at the last minute the buck veered away from me, never slowing down. I began to sit back down in the chair and then thought, "Wait a minute, what would make that buck panic?" I stood up again and just managed to see something jump aside as it was running toward me and crash into the vegetation. It kept running and continued to follow the buck. I immediately thought, "Was that a mountain lion?"

Another time I was sleeping on a cot in a campground after I had completed some bat fieldwork. I felt something breathing on the back of my head and turned to see what it was. A striped skunk had his front legs on the end of the cot and was staring at me. I carefully put my head back down on the cot and did what any sane, normal biologist would do: I went back to sleep. I never saw the skunk again.

Another time I was sprawled out on a long lawn chair watching an agave with night-vision goggles. I reached for my water bottle on the ground and heard a rattle. Was that a rattlesnake under my lawn chair? It was! I managed to launch myself into the air and as far away from the chair as I could. The lawn chair was old and there was a hole in the seat, directly where I was sitting. The rattlesnake was sitting right under my rear end! Once I got my wits together, I encouraged the snake to move on and resumed my observations.

Rattlers live in the desert too!

Fieldwork is very exciting, and there is never a dull moment!

11. As a Researcher in the Desert Southwest, You Probably Encounter Lots of Wildlife. What Kinds of Critters Do You Encounter Relatively Regularly? Snakes, mosquitoes, scorpions, tarantulas, and others are a normal part of fieldwork. When in the field, you always want to be careful where you step, stand, or sit. In the field, I have been stung by mosquitoes and scorpions, and chased by bees. Snakes want to avoid you just like you want to avoid them. They are an important aspect of the environment and you always need to respect them.

Tarantulas are a very special treat and I love to encounter them in the desert. They rarely bite, as long as you don't try to touch them. Gila monsters are pretty rare, but they are really cool creatures.

Saguaro in bloom

I'm not a big fan of kissing bugs though. At night I can hear them approaching from their buzzy wings. You want to turn on lights and look for them. They can bite you and you never feel it. I'm one of those people who have bad reactions (swelling, redness, burning) to their bites and I have learned to wear long sleeve shirts and tuck the bottom of my pants into my socks. Bug spray does not seem to deter them. Avoid them if you can. Tarantula hawks have a nasty sting, but you rarely get stung if you don't brush up against them or touch them. I got stung in the field once just by brushing up against a bush. The tarantula hawk did not appreciate it and stung me. All of these creatures are a part of the Sonoran Desert and very much an important part of it. Respect them and leave them alone.

12. Tell Me About Your Research. What Bats Do You Study, and Why?
I have been conducting an ongoing research project at the Chiricahua National Monument and Fort Bowie National Historic Site in the mountains of southeastern Arizona for the last 20 years. My bat research project at Tumacácori National Historical Site is in its sixth year. I am monitoring the bats in these

mountains for species diversity, tracking their movements, and evaluating their general health. I also check for any sign of White-Nose Syndrome (see page 25), since this deadly fungus has not shown up in Arizona at this time. I train federal employees at the National Park Service on the proper protocol for handling bats and studying them. Arizona has 28 species of bats and I have handled and studied 26 of them. I have also carried out research in northern Arizona and throughout the Mexican state of Sonora. I have carried out bat research on behalf of Luke Air Force Base, the Arizona Game & Fish Department, the Arizona-Sonora Desert Museum, and the University of Arizona. These research projects involved bat movements, effects of military jets on feeding, migratory movements, bat house occupation, and agave foraging by nectar bats. On a natural history trip to Costa Rica, I worked with a well-known bat biologist for several evenings netting bats.

13.   As a Permitted Wildlife Researcher, You Help Rehabilitate Bats at Your Home. Tell Us About the Bats at Home. What Are They Like? Do They Have Names?

A bat in captivity

Over the past 25 years, I have held non-releasable bats as educational ambassadors. The Arizona Game & Fish Department has issued me an educational permit to hold these bats as educational animals. The bats are the property of the Arizona Game & Fish Department. None of the bats can be released to the wild because they were born in captivity or have injuries. The bats are utilized at festivals, special events, educational presentations, and in live-animal demonstrations. I currently have two bats that I keep at my home. One is a 16-year-old big brown bat that I received when he was 5 months old, and his name is Kama. The other, Lester, is a pallid bat that I have had for 6 years and he came to me with a wing injury. He was an adult when I got him and I don't know his actual age. I have also had a canyon bat, western yellow bat, California leaf-nosed bat, and several other pallid bats. Their names included Lyle, Leta, Pip, Lily, and Mac.

14. What's the Biggest Thing I Can Do To Help Bats? Bats have a bad reputation, and that's not fair. Anything that you can do to dispel this myth would be helpful. Educate yourself by attending bat-friendly events and local workshops. Organize a bat-house (page 90) building event and install bat houses. Attend a local event that houses bats, such as those near bridges (page 98), and observe the bats as they exit the bridge at night. Pass on the word that bats are essential to our environment and our friends!

15. What Worries You Most About Bats and Their Future? I worry about climate change, ignorance, greed, excessive consumption, White-Nose Syndrome, and the future of bats on this continent.

16. Tell Me About White-Nose Syndrome. Just How Bad Is It? White-Nose Syndrome (WNS) is a cold-loving fungus that has killed more than 5.5 million bats in the eastern U.S. and is slowly spreading south and west. It has also been detected in Canada. The fungus usually affects bats that are in their winter hibernacula. The fungus forms on the bat's face, causing the bat to wake up from its winter sleep, burning important fat reserves; this eventually kills the bat. This disease has been devastating to bats and is the biggest threat to their health and welfare. Worse yet, the disease threatens species that already are endangered. Research continues on finding a cure to this disease. Progress has been made, but additional work is necessary.

A bat with White-Nose Syndrome (USFWS, Marvin Moriarty)

17. Is Climate Change a Problem for Bats? Climate change will affect every animal on Earth. We are already seeing big changes with birds and mammals. As areas warm, animals learn to adapt or they die. Other weather events kill animals directly, by flooding, fire, or via other weather extremes. Climate change includes drought, hurricanes, tornadoes, flooding, warming, and cooling. Bats are now being affected by drought, fire, and other events. The ability to fly gives bats an advantage to a certain degree, but even that has its limits. Bats can only fly so far and for so long.

18.   How Have You Seen the American Southwest Change Over Time?

My 20-year bat study at Chiricahua National Monument provides a good example of how things are changing in the American Southwest. I began this research project in 2000 and at that time I had six study sites. All of these study sites had a source of water (Bats are easier to capture when there is a water source available). Bats capture insects at the water, drink the water, and use water drainages as highways to travel from one place to another. Since 2000, three of my study sites have completely dried up. Even when we have a wet winter and a good monsoon season in Arizona, the sites do not hold water for any period of time. Arizona is experiencing a long-term drought, and this is a good example of the effects of climate change.

As climate change worsens, Arizona's already serious droughts will likely worsen

The fires in Arizona have also affected bat numbers and species. Drought and fire destroys bat habitat and roosting areas. I am no longer capturing certain bat species that I once captured in the past. On the positive side, the fires have also opened up areas for certain species of bats that weren't present in the past. Some of the larger, long-winged bats cannot fly in heavily vegetated habitats, and the fires have opened these areas to these species.

19. How Many Bat Species Have You Encountered Yourself? Do You Keep a List?
I have never counted the total number of bats that I have encountered, but I have handled 26 of the 28 species of bats in Arizona. In Mexico, I have handled 15-20 additional species, and when I was in Costa Rica about 20 additional species. Since there are about 1,300 species worldwide, I have barely scratched the surface!

20. OK, So You Study Bats. One Last Question: Who Is Your Favorite Superhero or Superheroine?
I would have to honestly say that Batman and, of course, Batgirl are my favorites! What else can I say? Spock from *Star Trek* is my science-fiction hero! He probably loved bats too!

WEBSITES:

These websites will help you get acquainted with resources on bats.

Bat Conservation International—www.batcon.org

Lubee Bat Conservancy—www.lubee.org

Bat World Sanctuary, Inc.—www.batworld.org

Bat Conservation Society of Canada—www.cancaver.ca/bats/canada.htm

Neighborhood Bat Watch—batwatch.ca/sp_canada

READING LIST:

These books will help you continue to learn about bats.

Adams, R. A. *Bats of the Rocky Mountain West: Natural History, Ecology, and Conservation.* University Press of Colorado: Boulder. 2003.

Barbour, R. W., and W. H. Davis. *Bats of America.* University Press of Kentucky: Lexington. 1969.

Fenton, M. B. *Bats.* Facts on File: New York, 1992.

Harvey, M. J., J. S. Altenbach, and T. R. Best. *Bats of the United States.* Arkansas Game & Fish Commission: Little Rock. 1999.

Hill, J. E., and J. D. Smith. *Bats: A Natural History.* University of Texas Press: Austin. 1984.

Monday, D. C. *Arizona Wildlife Views: Bats of Arizona.* Arizona Game & Fish Department: Phoenix. 1993.

Nagorsen, D. W., and R. M. Brigham. *Bats of British Columbia.* UBC Press: Vancouver. 1993.

Nowak, R. M. *Walker's Bats of the World.* The Johns Hopkins University Press: Baltimore. 1994.

Schmidly, D. J. *The Bats of Texas.* Texas A&M University Press: College Station. 1991.

Tuttle, M. D. *America's Neighborhood Bats.* University of Texas Press: Austin. 1988.

Wilson, D. E., and S. Ruff. *The Smithsonian Book of North American Mammals.* Smithsonian Institution Press: Washington, D.C. 1999.

INDEX

U.S. Fish & Wildlife Service, 98
U.S. Forest Department, 98

V
vampire bat, 26, 29
vision/eyes, 18, 28

W
Western long-eared myotis (*Myotis evotis*),
  68–69, 95, 104
Western mastiff bat (*Eumops perotis*), 86–87,
  105, 110
Western red bat (*Lasiurus blossevillii*), 50–51,
  95, 103
Western yellow bat (*Lasiuris xanthinus*), 62–63,
  104
White-Nose Syndrome (WNS), 25–26,
  115–116
wings, 14–15

NOTES